Foreword by the editor:

Mark Pennock-Purvis was my husband Mark's grandfather. He wrote this account shortly after his escape and I have turned the sheets of foolscap paper into this book in order to make his fascinating story available to family, friends, and others who may be interested a hundred years later.

All profits from the book will go to Starfish Zambia. This is a charity my husband has set up, to provide college education for young orphans in Zambia (where he grew up). This enables them to become teachers, mechanics, and nurses where otherwise they wouldn't have the opportunity to do so. For more information visit www.starfish-zambia.org

Carolyn Sheircliff

May 2018

ABOUT THE AUTHOR

Mark was born on 7 August 1897 in Whitby, to Elizabeth Pennock and John Purvis. He was the eldest of 9 children. John was a labourer, poorly paid, and fond of drink, so there was little money to feed and clothe the family. Mark got a job wherever he could (even before he left school), working as errand boy, caddie for golfers, and "Boots" at a local hotel.

In 1914 aged 17, he joined the Whitby Territorials and moved away to camp with them when the 1st World War broke out. He asked his parents to sign that he was 18, as he wanted to go with his friends. He served through to the end of that war, was wounded, awarded the Military Medal, taken prisoner, and escaped.

In 1921, Mark moved to Hungerford and enlisted in the RAF. He had reached Squadron Leader status when he retired in 1952.

He married Winifred Gingell in 1930 and their first child, Jane, was born in 1932. When Jane was 5 years old, Mark was posted to Malta and the family moved out there, where they had a son, Alan, in 1938. They returned to Hungerford at the start of the 2nd World War, where they had their 3rd child, Edna. Mark went on to serve in Germany and finally in Andover.

Mark was very much a "man's man" who represented the RAF at boxing and had many hobbies and interests, including amateur dramatics which he did in the Forces and afterwards. He enjoyed a few drinks and a cigar. He had a keen mind as can be seen from the quality of the writing of this account, describing life in a prisoner of war camp and his escape on his 21st birthday, 7 August 1918. Mark died in 1983 in Hungerford.

CHAPTER 1

I was just turned 17 when the Territorial Division, with which I was serving as a gunner in the Royal Field Artillery, was sent to France, in 1915.

Our "baptism of fire" could certainly be termed a thorough one, as the first engagement in which we took part was the second Battle of Ypres, (an engagement which cost us pretty dear) and I was in each action with my battery after that, until I was transferred to the French Mortar Batteries about a year later. I served in this branch from May 1916 onwards with a good share of adventure and a good share of luck and no more serious consequences than one or two slight wounds and several doses of gas (only one of which could be considered severe), until we ran up against it good and strong on the CHEMIN DES DAMES in May 1918.

This was the occasion of another of the big German drives that were the last convulsive throes of a beaten nation making a last desperate bid to turn the scale in its favour.

The offensive was carried out on similar lines to the previous ones, commencing with the one on the FERONNE front in March, and a piercing of the Allied lines was effected at two points, some eight or nine miles between, along a sector known as the "CALIFORNIA" PLATEAU. The first move being to take SOISSONS, RHEINS, FISMES, and several other places of importance on that front, with PARIS itself for the ultimate goal.

At that time our Division was holding that part of the plateau immediately in front of the ruins of what had been the village of CRAONNE, and our position was regarded as an almost impregnable one. It was about the centre of the frontage affected by the "push", and the plateau itself was honeycombed with saps and underground machine gun nests.

Here, it seemed, was a "cushy" sector at last, and most of us had settled down to a welcome spell of "peaceful" warfare, after many months of pretty hard going in most of the "hot-shops", stretching from Ypres right down the line.

It came as a very rude shock to most of us with that idea however, when, after the preliminary bombardment before what was to be another big enemy advance had ceased to batter our lines, (and we were telling each other that the enemy would soon know for certain that there was "nothing doing" in our direction), we looked back over the country behind us, in the early morning light and found it dotted with companies of Germans coming back to collect us. Whilst miles away behind us, in territory we had imagined was our own, observation balloons bearing the black cross that was the German aircraft identification mark, were being sent up to join the crowds of enemy planes that were already careering about and occasionally swooping down to empty their machine guns on whatever target was presenting itself.

There could only be one result, under the circumstances, and though we tried to fight our way out and adopted every resource to avoid capture, we ultimately found ourselves, a few hours later, being marched away behind the lines, stripped of our arms and possessions, (save the

clothing in which we stood), to some unknown
destination, to start upon a new phase of war-time
military experience - prisoners of war.

CHAPTER 2

The prisoners resulting from the drive, over 50,000 in number, were taken to various points behind the original German lines in that zone, and installed in "KOMMANDOS" each numbering about 2000 roughly, in wired-in corrals waiting to receive them.

Our idea, naturally, was that we should be transported, as facilities arose, to Germany, to be interned there in properly appointed prison camps and employed by our captors on non-military labour until the cessation of hostilities and subsequent repatriation, but we were soon to have that idea shattered.

The Germans were evidently using all their available manpower in the carrying out of their offensive and we were required for the work of reconstruction behind their lines, which included the making of roads and the laying down of railroad tracks over the territory gained, and developing the lines of communication and transport between the advancing armies and the bases. We discovered that quite a large number of Russian and French prisoners were already "caged" there, and some of us began to entertain both fears and hopes, having heard something about the way prisoners employed behind the lines were treated. However, we were never sent near enough to the front line to permit of opportunities to make a dash to re-join our own side, so our hopes of regaining our liberty through chances offered in this direction died out as time wore on.

For about the first four weeks of captivity I was employed in labouring work around the district of CRAONNE, being one of a party of about 2000 who were caged on the fringe of a small wood, close to where our old billets had been when we were in the trenches. There were no housing structures of any sort and when our days' work was over, we just had to throw ourselves on the ground and talk in little groups among ourselves until darkness set in and then fall into some sort of sleep until morning.

We had no blankets or overcoats, nor had the majority of us any kit of any description, and we couldn't get any.

Scarcity and poorness of food was another unfortunate condition to which we had to adapt ourselves. A loaf of black bread, about 2 ½ lb in weight, (and in many cases half rotted with mould), was served to each man to last him three days. Dinner consisted of one ladle-full of soup made from preserved vegetables, whilst for breakfast and tea each man received about a pint of "substitute" coffee and a small allowance of jam or grease.

It was starvation diet, but there was no use in rendering complaints, because the only answer we got was to the effect that we were lucky to get anything at all.

CHAPTER 3

After we had completed the work to be done in that area, we were transferred to the main prisoner camp of the area, which was situated at ST ERME, about sixteen miles further back, in the direction of LACH and our concentration camp at the time of capture.

There were several "KOMMANDOS" here, each in its own pen and we learned that there had been no consignments to Germany, excepting officers, since our detachment, nor had there been any facilities granted for the writing of letters.

Not once during the three months that I was a prisoner were any of us allowed to write, with the exception of a sort of Field Service Post Card, with which we were issued when it could be seen that everyone was becoming restless. These were served out one to each man, as the result of an application to the Kommandantur of the district, and each card showed "LIMBURG" as the place of our incarceration.

These cards, after filling-in, were collected by our jailers but were never despatched. It was never intended that they would be.

The CRAONNE detachment were soon to discover that life in this Camp was to be even harder than it had been in the one they had just left. Working parties were required in dozens of places, for divers purposes, chief of these being the development of the ST ERME Railway Station as a railhead, and our camp made up one of the working parties employed on this work.

Our working hours were from dawn until dark and we were driven like slaves. Any slackening of effort was rewarded by a blow or a kick, (our captors were in the position to do anything they liked with us, there being no-one to look after our welfare) and it was a thoroughly exhausted party that would painfully wend its way back to the compound as dusk set in.

In the matter of housing we were worse off than we had been in the old camp, for there we did have the grass to lie upon, whereas in this case we were compelled to lie on the bare ground, as the compound merely consisted of a cordon of wire set up around the ruins of two or three houses.

The food was worse here too, if anything, and one could feel oneself physically weakening more and more as the days passed. To make matters worse, disease was beginning to establish itself amongst us and dysentery cases were daily finding their way into a separately wired off part of the camp, (the ruins of what had been another house standing in its own bit of ground), which served to answer the purpose of a hospital. (It must be said here that a man had to be in a bad way before he was sent to the "KRANKENLAAGER" and he was fortunate if he came out again alive). Most of the prisoners in our compound contracted dysentery sooner or later, in varying stages of severity and as we possessed only the clothing that we stood up in, (which in many cases was scanty – several of us in my Trench Mortar Unit were wearing only khaki cotton shirts and khaki drill shorts at the time of capture), the rest can perhaps be guessed. In many cases where the nether garments were rendered quite useless and unsafe through the disease, they were discarded by the wearers and it was quite a common sight to see a man naked except for a tunic, (indeed, one man had nothing at all to wear save an old corn sack, in the end) and his boots.

A wash was a very infrequent treat, with never less than six or seven days between, and there was no soap, whilst the same filthy handkerchief served to dry a party of six or seven or more. We could not get a bath during the whole of the time I was a prisoner, and all through that period we never once had our clothes off.

Meat and fatty foods were amongst the things that remained memories only and so the horrible existence dragged itself along. The routine never changed - it was slave driving all the hours of daylight and penned in at night like utter beasts, tortured in mind and body alike, to get what rest we could for our wearied and exhausted frames under the totally unsatisfactory conditions afforded before dawn again announced itself.

The one bright spot in the whole nightmare existence lay in the fact that it very seldom rained.

The days were extremely hot. Sometimes the heat was scorching and the heavy choking dust, (all the vehicular traffic was of solid tyres, even to the bicycles, and as a consequence the roads were ground to powder), was at most times almost unbearable, but wet weather would have been infinitely worse, clad and housed as we were, and for this solitary comfort we were extremely thankful.

CHAPTER 4

After I had been in the ST ERME "KOMMANDO" about three weeks and a prisoner close on two months, a friend of mine who was a brother N.C.O (I was a corporal at this time) secured me a "staff job" in his party.

This was with the water wagon, and the party was employed on a permanent fatigue to keep the camp supplied with water for cooking purposes.

The wagon consisted of a large metal barrel, with a holding capacity of approximately 200 gallons, mounted on wheels, and with shafts to which a horse could be harnessed under the usual mode of transport. In this case the wagon was man-handled by the water party, (which consisted of ten men, including the two corporals), by means of drag ropes, and as there were a few hills in the district, the work was heavy.

There were three walls at different points of the village, all within a half mile radius of the camp, and to ensure an adequate supply of water, about four journeys had to be made in a day. The wagon was filled by buckets drawn up from the wells, which were very deep, and full grown men received a surprising and painful lesson in how heavy an ordinary bucket of water can be.

However, this work was more to be desired than employment with the main working parties, as there was change and movement in it. Also for the fact that it wasn't considered necessary to have a guard accompany the party, frequent rests could be taken without fear of bullying and ill treatment from our brutal gaolers.

It was however, far from this reason alone that I was glad and very eager for the chance to work on the water wagon. From the very moment of capture the idea of escape had never left me and almost every night I would lie awake trying to think out a suitable scheme.

Whilst working with the CRAONNE detachment I had made two abortive attempts, both of them meeting with frustration through insufficient knowledge on my part of the country immediately surrounding the camp, and this was a handicap I was determined to wipe off before making another attempt.

My new employment offered me many opportunities of exploring and becoming acquainted with the environments of the camp, and every point of entrance and the surroundings of the village were religiously noted and committed to memory, to be used when the chance came, as I was sure it would come – some time.

I stayed on the water wagon for a fortnight and then invited the "sack", which wasn't long in coming.

A new plan had suggested itself to me, and the apparently foolish idea of losing one of the best jobs in the compound was part of it.

CHAPTER 5

Having secured all the information there was to pick up about the situation of the camp and the village, the water fatigue was of no further use to me and the next move was to be placed on the main working party again. I schemed it that I became known to a few of the less surly of the guard, in order that as time went on, they would be less inclined to take notice of anything I did which might have attracted suspicious attention when practiced in the beginning. In this scheme I was successful. The main party from my camp was now being employed on the railhead again, and I made it my business each day to plant myself right under the nose of one of the guard and work steadily away, (or make it appear that I was), all the time we were out.

After a time some of them got to notice me, and very often one or other would tell me to stop and take a rest and would talk to me, in a half-playful, half contemptuously baiting sort of way, with the limited English he may have succeeded in picking up.

This was another step in the right direction and meanwhile, I had succeeded in picking up another very valuable bit of knowledge.

Each morning, after the camp had been roused, the party would be led out of the gates on the road, where the men were formed up in fours, counted, (this constituting roll call) and detailed off in batches, usually numbering about 50, to each member of the armed guard.

This made it impossible for a man to get away whilst at work without it being discovered almost immediately, as each guard used to check the number of his batch several times a day. In any case, it was useless to attempt a breakaway in daylight, because it was utterly impossible to travel more than a few yards without running into one of the enemy. The procedure of checking and allocating jobs usually took about 15 minutes and I made a point of falling in without dawdling, so that I could use the rest of the time in looking round for a suitable "take-off".

After a while it became quite clear to me that the ideal place was a narrow opening in the row of ruined houses on the opposite side of the street, in which were billeted the guards.

This opening was almost opposite the gate of the compound and appeared to lead out on the countryside bounding the village. We were now nearing the end of July and I had noticed that slowly but surely the nights were drawing out and that it was scarcely dawn at 5am, which was the time we were fallen in on the road.

It was about the 1st or 2nd August when I was made to realise that if I didn't make my attempt soon, I would be deprived of the strength to do so.

CHAPTER 6

Work that day seemed to weary me very easily, and it would be near the middle of the afternoon when I straightened my aching back for another rest, (the task that usually fell to me consisted of the wielding of an instrument like a pickaxe, only with a wide blunt nose, the object of which was to pack small stones and earth under the sleepers when new rails had been laid down, to stabilise them), when I suddenly became sick and giddy, my senses left me and I fell like a log across the track.

How long I lay there I cannot guess, but when I came to myself again, it was to find a German soldier, (not a guard, but a member of one of the Labour Corps or Engineer units who ordered and supervised our labours), bending over me.

This man, a big hulking ruffian whose face alone supplied almost sufficient evidence to hang him anywhere, was accusing me of shamming and he commenced to threaten me. My blood boiled then – but not only on account of that. I had recognised this man as one who had played a particularly vile, despicable trick a week or two previously. He was one of a party or three or four who had raided a food truck that was one of a number drawn up in the siding, and when they had taken what they wanted they hit upon the bright idea, (knowing that the looting would be discovered in a very short time), of covering up their share in the business and escaping detection. Calling over a few of the prisoners who were working nearby, he motioned to them to get into the truck and help themselves.

17

The poor wretches, starved into a state very little removed from that of beasts, never paused to suspect anything. Their hunger swayed them and into the truck they plunged, fighting, and clawing each other in their frenzied attempts to get at the barley and meal and dried fruits which formed its contents. Then the dirty scoundrel calmly walked off to find a guard, whom he directed to the scene.

The result for all those caught was a flogging when they got back from the compound, which nearly killed them. I had seen the whole thing, but of course no-one took the slightest notice of me when I tried to tell the facts to the prison staff.

My disgust and loathing on remembering all this, must have been showing too plainly in my face as I looked at the man who was threatening me, because he suddenly swung his huge fist and catching me flush in the face, knocked me off my feet. I got up somehow and even in my weak, almost helpless condition was aiming to crack him over the head with my working tool, when a sudden flash of reason told me that that would be a senseless thing to do and that if I didn't quickly control myself and allow the matter to slide, it was good bye to my hopes of getting away and perhaps of even living longer.

Unfortunately however, I had gone too far with the effort and I could see in his face the intent to finish me off. He whipped up a bayonet and was about to lay me out when he was stopped by a guard, (the only man in the whole crew, with a spark of decency in him), who had just drifted onto the scene.

This guard was an elderly man of between fifty and sixty. I had been included in his batch of prisoners for several days and had acquired a bit of a liking for him, because he was one of the very few who allowed the men to take things steady. He had often given me his dinner because he didn't like barley soup and this formed the guards' dinner about twice a week.

My rescuer managed to smooth the incident over and noticing my exhausted condition he allowed me to stop working and sit down for the rest of the day.

The little affair however, had brought it home to me that very soon I would be breaking down completely and then it would be useless for me to entertain my further hopes of getting my freedom.

An attack of dysentery which had fallen upon me a few days before, appeared to me to be rapidly getting worse and I was suffering a great deal of pain most of the time.

Another thing that forced itself on my mind as I sat and pondered, was the fact that my boots were almost finished and that very soon I should be bare footed; a state of affairs that was going to make my task more difficult. I had been wearing a pair of new boots at the time of capture, but twice had I been compelled to suffer a change in the very effective way that was adopted whenever one of our captors desired a change of footwear.

The obtaining of boots, (and in fact, anything at all), was a difficult matter for the German Army at that stage of the war, and as the British Soldiers' boots were so much better that their own, (substitutes were being used in every branch of the industry), they were far more to be desired. The common procedure was this; a German soldier seeing a prisoner with a better pair of boots than he himself was wearing, would draw the prisoner aside into a quiet place, take off his own boots, lay four or five cigarettes, and a hunk of bread beside them and stand waiting. The hapless prisoner soon realised that the political thing to do was to accept the "exchange" and the matter was settled. This little stunt had been worked on me twice – on the first exchange I got a pair that weren't quite so bad, but on the second I touched for a pair that had very little to separate the ground from the polish and after a fortnight's possession of my latest bargain I was faced with the knowledge that they hadn't much more time to serve.

When I got back to camp that night I began to make the preparations for my intended dash.

CHAPTER 7

As soon as it became quite dark, I made my way to the ruins of a cellar, (for the greater part, the village was just the same as many others that had been seared by the flame of war – most of the building had been shattered and blown to the ground by constant heavy shelling, whilst the others were all in varying stages of wreckage and dilapidation, but always the cellars escaped), in which was confined a soldier of the R.E's named Sylvester (I believe that was his name). He had only recently been recaptured after a great but futile effort to escape, in which he had covered quite a distance from the occupied territory, (his objective had been Holland, which it was his intention to reach by first striking and following the Rhine and later, the Maas), being at liberty for a week or two.

The "KOMMA DA TUR" rewarded all unsuccessful attempts to escape in a fashion that was characteristic of the Hun. The unfortunate person was sentenced to either seven or fourteen days of solitary confinement, (usually in one of these cellars), during which he went three days without food, one day on ordinary rations, three more days without and so on.

Sylvester and another man who had been with him in his attempt to escape were undergoing either seven or fourteen, (I forget which), days of this pleasant treatment and it was at the very small opening that served for a ventilation hole for this cellar that I spent several hours in the night for the next few days, talking with them and listening to the account of their attempt and failure.

None of the enemy guards stayed inside the compound overnight, but the reason I had to be so very careful in my visits to the confined men was that if I were discovered by the camp "DOLMETSCEER", the news would be speedily conveyed to our gaolers. The "DOLMETSCEER" was a Jew with a thorough knowledge of German, who had been serving in a battalion of the Northumberland Fusiliers at the time of his capture. Presumably he had not long been enlisted then and the direction in which his sympathies lay was perfectly obvious to the men in the compound. Many of them knew to their cost that it was unsafe to say things in his hearing that would not be favourably received by the enemy. Once we had the unpleasant experience of standing on parade in the compound whilst one of our number, who was called out in front by the Unter-Officer of the Guards, was brutally hammered because of some report that had been made by this person of doubtful nationality - yet possessed of the ability to speak German and English with equal fluency and who was a private in a British Regiment.

There were no restrictions on the movements of this man, (the handling of whom, it was announced to us on a full muster parade, by any of the prisoners would call down drastic reprisals from the prison staff) and his time was divided between the guards billets and the compound.

It would have bought trouble on the occupants of the cellar, as well as myself, to be discovered in one of these midnight discussions, so caution had to be the first law.

From Sylvester I learned a deal more about the surrounding country and from him I received the definite assurance that it was utterly useless to attempt escape into neutral territory by working toward the interior.

This had been my conviction all along, because after serious consideration had been given to the tremendous distance to be covered and the innumerable obstacles to be overcome, together with the fact that the whole country would be swarming with troops for very many miles, it was expecting too much from providence that anyone who had been weakened for months by starvation and disease should have sufficient strength to achieve such a stupendous feat.

Of course we had no idea as to the position of the trenches at that time, but I reckoned that I couldn't be much more than 50 miles away. Anyway, the distance to the Bay of Biscay itself must be much less than it would be to Holland, considering the route one would have to take.

When I told Sylvester that I intended to make a dash towards the firing line, with the hope of having the luck to break through, he was fully in support of the idea, because, (as he said), although the risk would be far greater and the penalty of failure would almost certainly mean death, the distance was shorter and the chances of getting through, especially if hard fighting were in progress, were far and away more to be fancied than those of obtaining freedom in the way they had tried.

The next movement was to find someone who would throw in his luck with me and I spent a couple of days in sounding a few of the men I knew personally; those particular ones who I knew from past experience of them would be the most likely men for the job. I had asked Sylvester what he thought about it, telling him that I would hang on for him until he had finished his term of confinement, but though the spirit was right there, it was beyond the power of the flesh to respond. "It's no good, old chap", he said, "I'd be so much luggage for you. I'm going down fast and I'm doubtful if I'll get out of this alive".

I never saw Sylvester again, but I've always had the earnest hope that he came through alright. He was game all the way.

From all the others I approached, the answer was the same. They were too far gone. Steadily encroaching physical weakness had robbed them of all their hopes and I realised that I would have to play a lone hand, after all.

CHAPTER 8

Then came the event that definitely decided the issue. In the early hours of the morning of 5th August a number of the Allies' planes flew over and dumped loads of bombs all around the village.

Everyone was roused by the explosions and the hubbub created by the Germans, who were scurrying around the street in utter panic. Although there was the chance that any minute a few bombs might fall into the compound, we were as elated as schoolboys and shouting our encouragement to the raiders to wipe the village off the map. The German guards got the wind up and we were told that if anyone showed a light, there would be summary action taken on the instant.

The raiders retired at last and, strangely enough, though bombs had been spilled all over the place, not one had dropped near enough to the compound to be any damage. However, we were soon to learn the extent of the damage caused during this surprise attack.

At dawn we were let out on to the road and marched off to work on the railhead as usual. On this occasion I was near the rear of the column and as we turned a corner into the straight stretch of the Station, we came upon a large hole and the remains of a transport wagon and horse team that been passing over that part of the ground just as the hole was made.

Of the team, there was practically nothing left but bones and bits of harness. The head of the column of prisoners had come across the scene and at the sight of real meat lying about spare, the starving and famished mob broke into a wild rush which was beyond the power of the guards to check. They fell upon the carcasses of the dead team with whatever implement they could find and, frantic with the pangs of hunger that had suddenly intensified, they hacked and tore until the guards got together at last and drove them off.

The Germans themselves were also badly in need of meat. However, a few of the prisoners got away with various chunks of flesh and the offal, which they were allowed to keep. It was a curious spectacle, the sight of a bunch of gaunt, emaciated wrecks, hairy, half naked, and unclean, clutching in their filthy hands those ragged hunks of bleeding horse flesh. The real sight was waiting at the railhead for us. There had been a large number of direct hits there and the damage was enormous and it was still going on.

A huge convoy of ammunition trucks had been drawn up in the siding over-night, prior to being despatched to the line the following day. At four points in the length of the train a direct hit had been registered and the result was havoc. Trucks were mangled and shattered, debris was everywhere and hundreds of live shells of every calibre had been thrown and scattered all over the place. Some of these were going off at intervals, and a cluster of hospital marquees that had suddenly sprung up nearby were doing a roaring business.

Parties of Germans were hard at work clearing away the wreckage and unloading trucks that were either smouldering or in danger of catching fire, but when the casualties began to increase, the subordinates flatly refused to go on with it. The result was that the British prisoners were set to work on it and when we held back and tried to protest we were told that if we didn't obey orders we would be shot. Things happened that day with a vengeance. Every now and then as a party would be empting the deadly contents of a mutilated truck, an explosion would occur and they would be seen to rush back to a safe position where a group would collect round the latest victims.

Two or three of my party, (I had been detailed to superintend the working of a squad of fifty or sixty men), were among the early cases and one was so badly smashed up that he lived only a few minutes. However, whilst he lay there in his dying struggles, one of the German labour party, (who was looking on from a safe distance), came up, removed the dying man's boots, and calmly walked off with them. Some of us felt a bit sick about this, but of course we couldn't do anything.

Before the morning was very old, my party had suffered quite a number of casualties, so the remainder were sent back to the compound, where they were employed for the rest of the day in any odd fatigue that could be found.

CHAPTER 9

So far I had had no luck in my search for a companion, nor had I been allowed the slightest opportunity to break away.

Realising that the position had now become a desperate one, I made up my mind to jump for it early in the following morning, as we waited in the faint light of breaking dawn to be marched off to work.

The happenings of the day were gloomily reviewed that evening amongst little groups of prisoners and the common question openly voiced was, "whose turn next?" I was determined it would not be mine and settled down to wait for the dawn. During the night there happened a sad sequel to the incident of the morning, when the dead horse team had been discovered and cut up. A few of the fortunate ones who had succeeded in getting away with pieces of flesh, had procured an old bucket, "pooled" their portions and stewed the lot for several hours. Then they gathered round and devoured their first real meat meal since being taken prisoners.

Ravenous with hunger, they ate until their jaws were tired. Early next morning, two of them were found to be dead. The heavy gorging of the rich food, to which their stomachs had become unaccustomed, had proved too much for their weakened systems and had killed them.

When morning came, I found myself again out of luck. The guards patrolled up and down the ranks as we stood waiting to be marched off and at no time was one of them more than a couple of yards from me.

This day, 6th August, proved to be a repetition of the foregoing one. We were again employed in highly dangerous work with the ammunition and the list of victims soon began to swell again. That day I lost one of my best friends, a corporal who had served in the trench mortars with me and who had seemed in the old days to bear a charmed life. A shell exploded whilst he and a few others were carrying it away and he was instantly killed.

As we pegged at our hazardous job, my brain was working overtime to devise some manner of slipping the guards. At last I got what seemed a good idea and I commenced to put the plan into action right away.

My attack of dysentery was by this time pretty bad and I hadn't a deal of trouble in persuading the guard, after I had reported it to him, to send me back to the compound, where I should be examined and, if considered ill enough, (which I knew I was), sent into the hospital camp.

This camp, as previously explained, adjoined the compound, being separated from it only by a wall about 6 foot high, running along the top of which were two or three strands of barbed wire.

When men were admitted to the hospital, their numbers were deducted from the strength of the compound and my plan was to get myself admitted, climb back into the compound through the night, and join the working party on the road the next morning. I planned to hang back in the gateway, until the men already formed up in fours were near to the gap between the houses that I had previously noted and then walk out when my position would be alongside the gap.

I could then slip away during the check, before the person who was counting got down to where I was. The check would be found correct and the strength of the camp accounted for, but I would be clear away and if my break was successful I would have a day's clear start before I was missed, as the roll of the hospital patients was checked in the evening.

CHAPTER 10

I was admitted to the hospital although it seemed unlikely I would be and I received my examination in the compound, because it seemed I was considered capable of two or three more days work before the dysentery would throw me over on my back.

However, the exhibition of a poisoned finger that was already badly swollen and festered, turned the scale in my favour and off to the hospital camp I went.

The game had started, and as I was being handed over to the sentry on the hospital camp gate to be passed through, my confidence in the ultimate success of the scheme increased with every step I took. When I got inside the camp, I made my way to the doctor, a little Officer of the American Medical Service who for months had been carrying on there with very limited supply of drugs and medicines allowed him, (even the few bandages supplied to him were of paper). He attended the ever increasing cases of sickness and disease, when he himself needed the attention of a doctor as much as anyone. He was as sick and ill as the majority of his patients and was kept just as short of the necessities of life as they were.

He gave me some medicine and told me to look out for a place to lie down in the "sick bay", which had been the upper floor of a wrecked building when the latter had been a house. He added that if I couldn't stand it, I was to come down and stay in the open air. I soon discovered the reason for this remark.

In the room above, lying about on the bare floor without a blanket or covering of any description, were dozens of sickness cases, nearly all of them dysentery in the worst stage and the stench was appalling. It was and had been for months, a veritable charnel house and it was easy to understand why most of the unfortunate wretches who went in there never came out again, (except to be deposited in a hole in the ground).

One in particular of the disease ridden men there arrested my attention and as I sat on the floor, nauseated, and almost suffocated with the vile odour of the place, I felt as if I couldn't take my eyes from him. The few filthy rags he was wearing hung loosely on his wasted frame and he moved about slowly and jerkily, as if by clockwork. As I looked at him I couldn't keep down the wave of horror that crept over me – he was a living, breathing skeleton. There wasn't a scrap of flesh on him and it was a deaths head that surmounted his shoulders, the skin being drawn tight over his bones and only the half dead eyes looking dazedly about him. I enquired his age from someone. He was 18.

There was nothing for me to do until night and darkness came, so I stayed there and I believe I hadn't the power to move away. I sat right close to the skeleton that was a man, whilst the day faded out and the dusk set in – just looking at him. Occasionally he spoke to two or three other men who had presumably been serving in the same company when captured, but each time the effort was a big one. Once I heard him say, "Well, here's one who won't get out of this. I think tonight will about see me off".

It did. He died just after midnight.

I crept down into the open air then, feeling horribly sick and wanting only to shut the sight of it all from my mind. Of the pictures that will stay in my mind always, that one will loom the largest – the "hospital" that was a mortuary at the same time, with the stench that was every bit as deadly as a gas-cloud, the revolting cases of disease, the gallant little gentleman, himself weak from sickness, struggling on in his attempts to bring them relief from their sufferings, further heavily handicapped by the insufficiency of remedial necessities – and a dead man walking about.

There was no moon that night, and when I guessed it to be somewhere around the small hours of the morning, I went to climb the wall back into the compound. I found I was unable to get a grip with my right hand, owing to the index finger having suddenly swollen to a huge size with the poisoned wound. It was causing great pain at the slightest touch. Tearing a strip from the leg of the old and tattered dungaree trousers I was wearing, (I had parted with my shirt and shorts several weeks before, and the dungarees had been acquired when discarded by one of the German Labour Corps), I soaked it with water, then I ripped open the swollen finger with a barb on the wire, and squeezed out all the foreign matter; afterwards tying it tightly round with the strip of cloth.

After a while the pain subsided and I was able to scale the wall, with its reinforcements of wire, back into the compound again. As I groped my way around, I came upon a group of men unable to sleep, sitting on the ground, and talking among themselves. Some of these knew me and when they asked why I had broken out of the hospital camp, I told them that I was leaving them that morning, as this was my 21st birthday, and I didn't like the idea of spending it in such surroundings. One of them said he wouldn't mind taking the chance himself and right away we formed a partnership.

It seemed curious that I should fall in with a partner right on the point of taking off, when I had spent days in a fruitless search for one, and it transpired that this fellow too had been looking around for quite a time to find someone ready to take the chance with him, with no more success than I had had.

I explained my plan to my new partner, (whose name was Isaac White, a Private of the Durham Light Infantry), although I had to add that the chance of a good start before our dash was discovered would be only a slight one now, as one of us would be missed at the check. I mentioned that I had become convinced that it would be useless to attempt anything else, so I had decided to head for the firing line.

He was full in agreement with this, and as we squatted on the ground in the darkness, we made all the final arrangements and rehearsed the first moves, while the others listened, occasionally giving us suggestions and wishing us good luck and success.

It came clearly to me as we talked, that in White I had found just the right man. He was in similar straits to myself, had arrived at the same desperate resolve for freedom whatever the cost, and he was equally determined, once clear of the hell we had suffered so long, not to be re-taken alive. With every minute I grew more eager for zero hour to come and the start of the attempt.

CHAPTER 11

It was just short of 5am when the guards came in to rouse the sleeping prisoners and we got up and stood near the partly sheltered section of the ruins where the German cook concocted the strange brew, (totally innocent of sugar or milk), that passed for coffee. A small quantity was given to each man before he set out on the road. We secured a little of this and retired to the rear of the compound to make the most of it, as for all we knew this would be the last warm drink for some time......and possibly the last we would ever take.

It was still dark, which cheered us up wonderfully, and the dawn hadn't broken when the guards commenced to hustle the party out on the road. Keeping to the letter of our plan, we hung about in the crowd, narrowly escaping being separated several times as the men surged around us, until the opportunity we were waiting for came. We pushed our way through the gate, crossed the road, and took our places in the party directly abreast of the gap that was our objective. There wasn't a second to lose, as the guards were already establishing themselves at intervals down the column, whilst the "Unter-Officer" passed along on his check.

We crept like rats into the dim shadows of the hiatus. A few yards along and a turn brought us round to the rear of the battered houses that lined that side of the street and as far as we could make out, we had to turn another corner to get into the open country.

As we crept stealthily along, trying to make our going noiseless, I heard footsteps behind and whispered to White to carry on while I made sure we weren't being followed. I waited round the angle of a wall as the person approaching came up. It turned out to be one of the Guards, who came along carrying his rifle at the trail. He almost fell on top of me and calling up all the strength I had left, I jammed my left fist into his abdomen. The man doubled up and grabbing at his bayonet, I lunged it into him as he crouched in the semi darkness. The weapon seemed to slip into his body curiously easily and he dropped without a sound. The struggle hadn't lasted many seconds and I hurried in the direction taken by my partner to find him waiting on the fringe of the ruins, with the open country beyond.

I didn't say anything to him then, but silently and quickly we hurried along over a small field, and crossing a ridge that left the village out of sight, we came upon an open stretch of what had been Orchard Lane, with a sunken road separating it from a small expanse of woodland. Stopping under a tree on which damsons were growing in fairly large quantities, we had commenced to fill our pockets with the fruit, when my dysentery pains came on with greater force, and the reaction of the excitement of the start settling in, I fell down at White's feet.

Minutes passed, during which I fought hard, urged by my partner, for sufficient strength to get to my feet, and reach the wood, where it was decided we should hide through the day. At last, driven to supreme effort by the realisation that it had suddenly become quite light and the knowledge of what was waiting if we were caught now and returned to the compound, I managed to stagger to my feet. However, we didn't move a step. Just at that moment a horse and cart driven by a German soldier came round a concealed corner on the sunken road just ahead of us. Had we been a minute earlier we would have come on to this road at the exact time that the cart turned into it. There was nowhere to turn for cover, so we just remained where we stood, afraid to move a muscle, and praying wildly that the driver would pass right by without noticing us. The heavy and ancient horse, plodding along at the slowest possible pace, seemed to take years to pass us and when it drew abreast of us as we stood there, not fifty yards away, I felt myself going dizzy with the strain. Our luck held and the cart went by without the driver as much as lifting his head and as soon as it had disappeared round a bend we made for the trees and the undergrowth in the fastest speed we could muster; the little incident having made us alive to the urgency of getting to cover before the enemy started moving about.

We entered the wood and roamed about in the search for a suitable place to hide until nightfall and presently we came upon a disused sand quarry with several caves which we commenced to explore. Among our few possessions, (which consisted of a rusty knife, a metal spoon, a broken penknife, two water bottles, a rusty old billy can, and a small pocket compass that wouldn't function), was an invaluable asset, contributed by White, in the shape of a spark igniting petrol charged cigarette lighter, of the type common among the troops during the war. By the aid of this we discovered that one of the caves was fairly deep, with tunnels branching off in different directions. In one of these burrows we lay down to sleep and wait for the arrival of darkness again so that we could resume our journey, as we knew that it would only be possible for us to travel at night and take our rest during the day. Before we went to sleep we congratulated ourselves and each other on our success so far and my partner also paid me birthday complements with the added remark that "perhaps it wouldn't be nice to wish me many happy returns of the day". I couldn't resist a grin as the grim humour of the situation struck me.

We dozed off, but I could only sleep in fitful bursts, the slightest sound serving to bring us bolt upright, with wide eyes staring into the black darkness, every nerve strained and breath coming in sharp little hisses.

I was suffering great agony and I told White that in case the disease increased upon me to the extent of keeping me off my feet he was to go right ahead and make the most of his own chance. This, however, he flatly refused to do, telling me that as far as he was concerned we would either sink or swim together. Then he succeeded in getting me off into a fairly long sleep, whilst he sat there for hours on the alert.

CHAPTER 12

When I awoke again, it was well on in the evening and I was feeling a great deal better and able to carry on. Strangely enough, after that night the dysentery left me and I was no further troubled by it.

We had to make several trips to the mouth of our cave to peer out into the night, before we decided that it was dark enough, (and late enough), to travel. When we were satisfied that it would be reasonably safe to start moving again, we emerged from the sand pit and cautiously worked our way to the fringe of the plantation. We looked about for the road that stretched from ST ERME through ST THOMAS WOOD to CRAONNE.

It was our intention to follow this road, (keeping parallel and well clear of it), as far as we could until dawn came. As we lay then, our position was somewhere to the right of this road. Our plan was to cross it and keep to the left, because the country on that side, as near as I could remember, was fairly clear of habitation, there being large tracts of marshy ground and wooded sections for quite a distance. We moved on until we came to a large open space, of about the same dimensions as a football pitch, with a bottle-neck entrance at each end and at the far side of which we knew was the road, flanked on the far side by wooded country again. Into this clearing we went, I taking the lead and White following up about a yard behind me. I hadn't proceeded 20 yards before I suddenly stopped dead and reached out to get a grip on White' arm.

There was no moon, but there being a few stars in the heavens, the night wasn't completely dark and things were dimly discernible up to a distance of ten or fifteen yards. I was staring at a large number of curious bulky heaps dotted all over the ground, and the reason for my abrupt halt was right at my toes – a number of rifles formed into a "pile", which I had all but knocked over. Looking at these and my eyes becoming sufficiently accustomed to the deep gloom to enable me to probe it, noticing that similar "piles" extended at intervals right down the clearing, the truth of the situation came to me like a flash.

We had stumbled upon the bivouac of a large body of troops, (probably a battalion on its way either to or from the front line) and I hurriedly whispered the news to my partner. It was necessary for us to reach the road, so there was nothing for it but to keep right on, (we would be running almost as much risk if we turned back now anyway), moving with the minimum of sound and trust to providence that none of the sleepers would wake, or that we wouldn't blunder into a sentry. Slowly and stealthily, with every sense alert, we made our way down the clearing, carefully avoiding the sleeping soldiers and the heaps of kit and arms. We afterwards mutually confessed that never under the worst shelling or firing had we been so shaky as we were when we stole like shadows through that sleeping camp.

Our marvellous luck remained firm. Evidently the soldiers were tired and worn out, as not a single one stirred, nor did we come upon any sentry and reaching the far entrance of the clearing, we passed through, found the road, crossed it, and gave great sighs of relief and thankfulness as we reached the woods on the other side.

We plodded on through the trees and shrubs, heading in the direction of CRAONNE, and ultimately we emerged from the wood at a point where it broke off into marshy district. The night was well advanced when we came abreast of the heap of rubble that had been CRAONNE, and often through the last two or three miles of our journey we had to make sudden quick dives to the left as we wandered too near to the road, on which Germans in ones and twos kept coming one way or the other all through the night.

On one occasion we got right onto the road and didn't realise our danger until a group of two or three of the enemy, evidently returning from the line, approached, and actually passed us before we could strike off to the marsh again without making it appear suspicious should we have been seen. The soldiers passed within a few feet of us and under the idea that we were two of their own people, even called out a greeting as they went on. (Needless to say they didn't get an answer – and they must have written us down as surly dogs).

CHAPTER 13

When we passed the ruins, I suggested to White that we find some place to rest through the coming day, as we had covered what seemed a good distance and there being no need to overdo it, our time being now all our own. He agreed to this, and we were just about to commence our search when he suddenly started and drew my attention to something that quite escaped me.

We had been following the single railway lines that in that place were running parallel to and about 50 yards from the road and just ahead of us, looming through the darkness were a number of trucks that had evidently been drawn up there for the night. Walking up to them, we started to scout around on the off chance of finding something, each of us taking a different point of the convoy to work from, there being about eight trucks in all.

The first two I examined were empty, but from the third one came a chorus of snores in varied chords and volume, telling me that troops were sleeping inside, and I retreated from that truck with far more speed than I had from the other two. I went along to find White, in order to pass the warning and found him looking at a shallow truck that was piled with boxes. (The German soldier carried his spare and private kit in a wooden box about the same size and after the fashion of an ordinary suitcase).

We retired a short distance to talk, as I didn't want to risk disturbing the sleepers, (though certainly not for their sakes) and I told him what I had discovered. He also had come upon a truck load of sleeping men, but in his case the truck was at the far end of the string. White then announced his intention of securing one of the boxes, in the hope of finding food in it and though I felt inclined to dissuade him, having the idea that we would be inviting extra risk, (we couldn't be sure that there wasn't a guard posted on the train), I fell in with his plan because our commissariat was somewhat short. In addition to the few damsons we had picked the previous morning, we had about a pound of black bread and we were heading in the wrong direction to allow of the assumption that nature would keep us supplied with food in the way of fruit and vegetables.

Back we went to the trucks and I kept a watch on the convoy with special eye on the occupied truck near the one we had designs on. White climbed into this and quietly removed one of the boxes, which he handed to me. I placed the box on the ground, a few yards away from the track, and then went back to collect another that my partner was holding ready. White then re-joined me on the ground and each catching up one of the boxes, we scuttled like rabbits for the marsh. Gaining this we slackened our pace so as to cause minimum of sound as we threaded our way through the dense growth of reeds, which rose to a height of about six feet. We must have penetrated these to a depth of several hundred yards before we came to a halt, panting, and sweating, on the edge of a good sized shell crater over which the growth was beginning to spread again.

Dawn was near at hand and here before us was a capital place to hide, so we dumped the boxes into the hole and soon scrambled in after them. Forcing open the boxes, we started to investigate the contents. In White's prize we found quite a number of useful things. These consisted of a heavy white woollen blanket, which was instantly called into service, about half a pound of tiny "iron ration" biscuits, a box of matches, three or four candles and a really priceless gift – five cigars.

The original owner of my box, a gentleman apparently accustomed to signing himself Herr Hillinghauser, had obviously been a thrifty sort of person, with a greater belief in laying aside for the future than in carrying stuff around with him. This was suggested by the presence in his box of three or four well stamped War Loan Cards and the absence of any useful items save an old safety razor, (we hadn't seen one for months) and two cigars.

The bulk of the contents of each box was made up of packets of old letters and sundry items of ladies fancy underwear; the latter evidently the proceeds of a little looting, that were being kept as presents for their women folk. In the way of men's underclothing, which we had confidently expected to find and of which we stood in great need, there wasn't so much as a pair of socks.

Discarding the ransacked boxes, which we covered with reeds, we settled down in the shell hole to make ourselves comfortable for the day, first making a "meal" of a small portion of our scanty stock of bread and a few mouthfuls of water which we had obtained from a spring in the woods.

CHAPTER 14

Before we turned to sleep we each lit up a cigar and enjoyed our first smoke in months. (Back in the compound all sorts of ideas were resorted to by smokers to evolve a working substitute for tobacco. A common practice was to collect a few leaves from the hedge, dry them over a fire, crumple them up, and roll the dust in scraps of old paper – until the paper ran out). We had to make our smokes last, so we regretfully put out our cigars after about an inch had been consumed, and covering ourselves with the blanket, we went to sleep.

We slept most of the day through August 8th and woke to find the sun edging over to the West. Not a soul had disturbed us, though as we could hear, plenty were moving about not far away and once a dog came very close to where we lay. However, it didn't get near enough to notice us, which was perhaps as well for all three of us, (White and I were each waiting with a hefty stick in our hands), and passers-by became less frequent as the evening wore on.

As soon as it was dark again, we climbed out of the shell hole, folded up the blanket, (which we decided to take with us, carrying it in turns) and set out to accomplish another stage of our journey. This time we kept well clear of the road, making our way through the reeds until the marshy district opened out into the country well clothed with trees and verdure, with intermittent stages of woodland.

On our way through a fairly large coppice we came upon another fresh water spring and from this we filled our bottles, after taking sufficient inside to satisfy a thirst of 10 or 12 hours standing. Though the shortage of food was serious, we weren't doing so badly for water, on the whole, and this was a big comfort as the weather was exceedingly dry and dust was heavy everywhere.

We travelled on through that night without incident of any sort and with not the least idea where we were going, being guided only by the occasional sound coming faintly in our ears of carts and wagons proceeding along the road, (which we left never less than a quarter of a mile to a flank).

My knowledge of the district had ended when we left CRAONNE behind, and our only course after that was to get right on until we came, in time, to heavy gun positions and other evidence of proximity of the firing line. Then we would only be travelling blindly after that until we would be able to hear the bursting of shells and later on, to see the "Verey's" lights at night, after which direction would be an easy matter.

CHAPTER 15

Just before dawn on August 9th, we arrived at the outskirts of a ruined village, the shell scarred houses of which were slightly less dilapidated than those of ST ERNE even, (though there was no signs of these being used) and we commenced to prowl around in search of another hiding place. Most of the ruins afforded no shelter whatever and we were walking down what had been the main street, taking a careful survey of the buildings on both sides, when we noticed with a sudden shock that it was almost daylight. The darkness had lifted incredibly suddenly and realising the situation and the urgency of getting under cover straight away, we started to move briskly.

We had just rounded a bend in the street when we got the surprise of our lives. Not more than 10 yards away from us, smoking and leaning against the battered gate of what had been a farmyard, was a German soldier. Luckily for us he was looking away from our direction and hadn't heard our approach, (to do this he would have needed sharp ears as we were by this time almost bare footed; the soles of our boots having almost disappeared) and we were back out of sight as swiftly and noiselessly as snakes before he could look round again.

As we doubled back, it became evident to us that others were moving about now and getting near to panic, we cut through to the outskirts. Here stood what had been a large house with the lower floor badly shattered and nothing remaining of the structure of the upper floor save the ragged skeleton of the wall, the farthest side, (away from the village), of which was completely missing. As we feverishly gazed up at it, it grew plain that this place would be as good as any. Nobody would dream of taking this heap of ruins as a billet – certainly not the upper part – and we straightaway entered and clambered up to the second floor.

The floor was fairly sound, though piled in places with debris and shattered masonry, but we picked out a corner that was fairly clear and in which if we laid down we would be out of sight of anyone below. Before settling down, we looked around to see if we could find anything useful and our search was rewarded with a couple of old and tattered German tunics which we promptly changed for our own, (the latter being long past their usefulness anyway) and an old German "pill-box" cap, which I took to go with the tunic, (also because I had not had a head covering since being taken prisoner).

We were now fairly well disguised, though I should think that we were certainly the weirdest looking soldiers ever seen in the German Army. We lay down in the corner to sleep, covering ourselves with the blanket, and then commenced to experience a day crammed with such a number of incidents, (so startling that even ourselves could hardly credit as really happening), that we were convinced that the God of Good Luck had specially adopted us for his own.

During the last few days our nerves had become tuned to a pitch similar to that possessed by wild animals. However long and deeply we could sleep if undisturbed, the slightest sound served to bring us wide awake and to the alert and we seemed to have acquired an extra sense by means of which impending danger would be communicated to us.

We were suddenly awakened from our sleep, (somewhere just short of noon we guessed it to be, as the sun was up and rather fierce), by the sound of someone ascending the broken rickety stairs and fully alert on the instant, we prepared for happenings.

Our visitor proved to be a young German soldier evidently filling in a spell of rest by exploring the ruins. He stopped just short of the floor and looked round and finally caught sight of us stretched out in the far corner. Standing there gazing at us, during which time we daren't move, he seemed about to say something, when suddenly he turned about and went down the stairs again.

We couldn't understand this, and affrighted at being discovered in daylight, our first thought was to make a dash for it, but we dismissed the idea as useless, knowing we wouldn't get far. As nothing immediately followed this incident and we began to calm down again, we gathered the reason for the silence and sudden departure of our visitor.

I was wearing the German "pill-box" hat, and as we lay on the floor with the blanket covering us to the chin, we must have presented ourselves to the German as two of his compatriots resting in what was apparently our own billet. To add to this impression, one of the German tunics was lying on the blanket and as he himself was evidently on the scrounge, he had realised that he was trespassing, and had accordingly made himself scarce.

We were thankful for the escape and knowing that we could expect more of these visits, we immediately proceeded to strengthen the appearance that we were a couple of real tired "Jerrys", just out from the line, but wearing the tunics and keeping the blankets tucked down so that they could be seen from the top of the staircase.

CHAPTER 16

My partner proved himself a real fatalist. He sat up and said, "Well, seeing that we don't stand much chance of getting a sleep, I think we'll employ the time in cooking a meal. You can imagine this to be "The Carlton Grill" and I'll be the head chef – though I don't suppose they turn anything out of their kitchen quite like the spread I am going to prepare". Then, arranging a few bricks at his side to form a fireplace, he passed me the broken pen knife, whilst he kept the rusty old table knife, and securing a few pieces of wood that had once been part of a door, we started to lay the fuel. I supplied the shavings and then spills to start the fire, and he hacked up the larger pieces to keep it going.

When the tiny fire was crackling away, he put some water from one of our bottles in the billy can, bumped in the remaining damsons and the small hard biscuits, and then busied himself with feeding the fire and attending to the cooking, whilst I cut up the chips of wood and eagerly awaited the result. I think the concoction took about three hours to cook, during which time we had several callers, most of whom went away immediately when they saw the room occupied, though a few were inclined to be further inquisitive.

There were two in particular who made themselves quite a nuisance. They became quite interested in an insolent sort of way when they noticed us lying there apparently worn out, with our little fire struggling to keep going and evidently their time was all their own because they sat down at the top of the stairs and showed no intention of going away.

After staring at us for a while, talking, and laughing among themselves as if at some joke, they tried to draw us into conversation. Naturally we didn't encourage this, partly because we didn't desire their company, but chiefly because neither White or myself knew more than six words of German.

We had to get rid of them somehow, so deliberately ignoring them, we turned on our sides and pretended to go right off to sleep. The idea succeeded. Our unwelcomed visitors continued to talk and laugh between themselves for a time, until seeing it was useless attempting to get us to join in, they slowly descended the stairs and left us alone again, thankful to have so fortunately come through the closest call we had had so far.

The two soldiers fired their parting shot from outside the building. We were just settling down again to wait for the next intruder when something whizzed through the air and fell on the floor close to my side. It was a bottle, thrown up from the ground below, and at first we thought we were booked for a little horse play in the shape of a bombardment of heavy stuff, but nothing else came and as soon as the merry guards had gone, I examined the bottle. It was full of petrol spirit, and presumably they had thrown it up to make our fire burn nicely.

At last White finished his culinary operations and although the result was a curious mess, to two starving men it was as acceptable as anything better and we ravenously devoured our first warm "meal" for three days.

We finished the feast off with a few whiffs of our precious cigars and twilight having now begun to set in, we were feeling a little more relieved and eager for the opportunity to quit our hornet's nest of a hiding place, when our last, and most frightening visitor came up. From his collar ornaments we could see that he was a senior N.C.O and he seemed more surprised than any of the others to see us there. Then he started to ask us questions and we saw trouble ahead.

Following immediately our previous plan, we turned over to sink back into a sleep apparently occasioned by sheer fatigue and I helped to make it a little more realistic by working up a groan of pain. Our fearsome caller seemed to be a little puzzled as to what to do, but he burst into a rapid flow of words from which I gathered that we were in the wrong department, that he was bringing a bunch of his own men round for billets that night and that we were to get out of it as soon as possible, (he needn't have worried about that part of it – we were frantically eager to get out of such a hazardous situation without being told). Having delivered himself of his little speech he took himself off, and some minutes later our pulses stopped their mad racing and came down to normal again.

CHAPTER 17

The happenings of that day just about unnerved us, and I had a horrible fear that if another German were to come up I should go right off into hysterics. However, no one else came to worry us, but we were feverishly impatient for darkness to come and when at last we could safely assay the departure, we were out of those ruins like frightened rabbits.

Skirting the outer edge of the village was a large hill, which from about a third of the way up was heavily wooded. At the foot of the hill were scattered two or three ruined houses and into that we strolled, on the off chance of finding something before setting out to tackle the wood. (It was certainly an off chance, because the most noticeable thing concerning billets or dug-outs vacated by "Fritz" was the total absence of anything useful. Whereas in any old place that had been occupied by any of the British Army one could usually fall across at least a tin of "Bully", the only thing that could be found lying about spare in German billets were empty cans. That was because they had so little for themselves).

In one of the ruins we entered, it seemed that the unusual had occurred. As we groped about in the darkness I nearly fell over a rough sort of table, made out of a packing case, on which were a number of cans. One of these fell on the floor and evoked a soft but emphatic curse from my partner and a whispered warning that there might be someone within hearing.

We discovered the cans to be some that had contained sausage and as we felt inside them there seemed to be a little left inside them. Without troubling to examine it, we started to claw the stuff out and cram it into our mouths, but wolfishly hungry as we were, we didn't take that first mouthful far. Sausage meat there certainly was inside those cans and also dozens of beetles and other insects. This was bad enough, but I had to travel nearly 200 yards to the wood before I could attempt to clear my mouth of the traces of that horrible stuff.

The dewfall was very heavy that night and as we made our way through the dense undergrowth of the wood, we were drenched through to the skin, (which wasn't far). It seemed as if we were booked to run up against a few snags that night, because on two occasions we arrived at a point which told us quite plainly that we had been wandering in a circle and that rather exasperated us.

Eventually however, we struck the right direction and came out on the other side to a large tract of fairly open country. We could now hear, far away in the distance, the faint booming of guns and this cheered us up immensely, as it brought us two valuable bits of knowledge; First, that the question of direction was now solved and second, that we were approaching the end of our journey.

Tramping along for two or three hours without incident, we came at last to a wide river along the bank of which we had to travel some distance before we came to a bridge. Now we had arrived at a perplexing situation.

I reckoned this river to be the AISNE, (which actually it was) and it only seemed natural to us that there would be someone on duty in the vicinity of the bridge, (either a watchman or guards) and we had to prowl about for some time before ascertaining that there was no-one at our end of it. To get to the other side we <u>must</u> cross by the bridge, because neither of us could swim a stroke, and for a good while we lay on the bank in puzzled silence wondering how we were going to accomplish it. Finally, hearing no sound from the other side, we decided to risk it, creeping stealthily along, clinging closely to the side of the bridge in order to leave the centre clear in case anyone should be looking along it, we slowly and steadily worked our way across. There seemed to be no one at the other end when we got over and we quickly swerved off into the unfrequented country again and wended our way onwards.

For some time we moved steadily along, noting increasing evidence of more life and activity with each succeeding mile that we covered, until we came to a high ridge that sloped down into a wide cutting, through the centre of which a road winded.

Down the side of the bank on which we stood, were two terraces formed by paths that ran parallel with the road. Making our way down to the first one, we travelled some distance along it, away from the sound of the traffic and other signs of occupancy, looking for some sort of shelter, as dawn was again near at hand. Ultimately we came upon a rough sort of funk-hole on the side of the bank which had evidently been dug when the allies held this district. Here we decided to pass the day, first collecting a lot of old brushwood and arranging it in a careless heap in front of the entrance to prevent any chance passer-by from seeing inside.

CHAPTER 18

Stretched out in the funk-hole and covered by a blanket, we ate the last small pieces of our bread and smoked for a few minutes, listening to the reports, at no great distance from us, of heavy guns firing, whilst we mapped out the remaining stages of our journey.

The guns firing in front of us I took to be 5.9's and I reckoned from this that we were now about seven or eight miles from the front line. The rate of going from now on would be naturally very slow, as we should have a much harder task to avoid coming into contact with enemy troops. The last mile or two would be swarming with them and much of our time would be taken up in dodging and lying low, so I figured it out that we had two or three more nights to travel still in front of us.

We decided to attempt to reach the Field gun positions with our next advance, after which we would get near enough to the trenches to enable us to take a good look round before essaying the final dash. The most serious question now was how much farther we could go without food and we knew that the answer to that was – not much.

We were almost mad with hunger and we had weakened to such an extent now that every mile seemed like ten and our legs dragged and ached. Lately we had been unable to proceed more than two miles without having to stop for a long rest and our position was getting serious. The bulk of our remaining strength would have to be saved too, to be used at the latter end in a culminating dash through the lines, and this and every other phase of the remaining stages was reviewed thoroughly, before our wearied bodies sank into a heavy sleep.

Light was streaming into our funk-hole through the brushwood screen when we again wakened, and the first sounds to catch our ears were the short reports of anti-aircraft guns, a number of which were pumping off their shells at some daring scouts that had managed to penetrate beyond the lines of trenches.

There is a strong fascination in the firing of an anti-aircraft gun. Almost everyone immediately looks up at the smoke puffs indicating bursting shells, to try to follow the flight and fortune of the observed invading machine, and the very first thought in our minds was to obey that same instinct. We crawled to the mouth of our funk-hole and were just going to pull the brushwood aside and peer out, when White suddenly put up a warning hand and flattened out, motionless. Following his example, I lay prone and followed the direction of his eyes as they gazed towards the entrance. As I leaned forward, the better to see through the brushwood, I caught a glimpse of something that almost made my heart stop beating for a second or two and then pump away so violently that I could have sworn it could have been heard yards away. Right there in front of our rough screen was planted a pair of spurred riding boots, over which appeared a pair of legs encased in riding breeches.

Minutes passed, during which my mind was too dazed to act, before, scarcely daring to breathe we crawled like a snake to the brushwood and looked out and up.

With his heels on the very edge of the entrance to our funk-hole and not ten feet away from us as we lay there motionless and sweating from the sudden shock, a German Officer was standing and focussing a pair of field-glasses on some point in the sky where the marauding plane was evidently disporting itself.

Silently and with our lungs almost bursting with the breath that we daren't yet exhale, we made our way back to the rear of the hole and in the time that followed I was reminded of the old saying that, "a watched kettle never boils".

The officer stayed right there for more than half an hour before he at last went away and left us to congratulate ourselves on yet another wonderfully lucky escape.

CHAPTER 19

Several times that day we heard footsteps passing the entrance to our hiding place and on one occasion someone, evidently with a view to using it for fire kindling, even took part of the brushwood away. When nightfall came, there was not the utter silence we had known on other nights. We were now in the district where troops would be moving about at all hours and we had to set out with the dark and take our chance, though we naturally took all precautions to avoid where there was most activity.

Our best plan after descending into the cutting, seemed to be to switch off to the left, in the hope of avoiding the road; and this we did. It didn't avail us much however, because we hadn't gone far, before, in descending one of the many ridges which seemed to abound in that district, we suddenly found ourselves in the middle of the road again. We were in what appeared to be a continuation of the cutting or sunken road we had come to that morning, when we stopped to find a hiding place.

The only signs of movement at the time were coming from behind us, so we decided to keep for a few minutes to the road, which seemed to be rising, and ascertain when we reached the crest of the slope, in which direction it would be safest to strike off again. The night was very dark and it was impossible to see for more than a few yards ahead, so our rate of travel was slow.

Turning a sharp corner in the road, we received a shock that brought us to a dead stop, and robbed us of the power to either move or think for several seconds. The cutting seemed to be packed with several men, all ranging up in ranks and standing to attention and the nearest file were less than half a dozen yards from us. In a cleared space in front of the company was standing a person, evidently a senior Officer, who was reading something out from a paper which he held in one hand, the other employed in holding up a hurricane lamp.

As our bewildered brains slowly cleared, we saw by the faint light from the lamp in front, that the company of men was a large one, filling the cutting as far down as visibility was possible. We turned to double back in our tracks, but it was too late. Small groups of soldiers were coming up behind us and there wasn't much time for us to act before they would be upon us. The only course open to us was to attempt to pass those in front and pray to our lucky stars that we would not be held up, so forward we went, hugging the bank as we marched on with our hearts bumping up against our back teeth.

In some places the rear rank of the assembled troops was so near to the side of the cutting that there was no room to pass and we had to force our way through, barging roughly into some of the soldiers and almost knocking them over.

The address they were listening to was evidently a very important one, because with the exception of one man who turned and half made a kick at us, they were far too interested to mind what we were doing. It seemed hours to our tortured minds before we came to the end of the ranks and a hundred yards further on we stopped an breathed freely again.

We had now arrived at the summit of the rise and as far as we were able to see, the country seemed to drop again to more or less a flat level. Leaving the road, we switched off to the right, but we hadn't gone very far when we were almost knocked down by a team of heavy draught horses dragging a limber, (sturdy two-wheeled carriage), of a heavy gun and followed closely by two more teams that had suddenly come up from behind us. We drew aside to let the procession go by and by reaching out a hand we could have touched the drivers as they passed.

About 20 yards further on they pulled up and from the sounds that followed it was quite clear to us that we had stumbled upon a battery in action. This meant another change of direction, so we went right off to the left again.

The new ground seemed not to be used quite so much as that we had traversed so far, the grass was fairly long and trees were scattered here and there. Far off in the distance, we could now see occasionally the faint illuminations in the sky that signified the firing of "Verey" light cartridges and we felt greatly cheered as we set our noses in that direction.

It must have been two or three hours later, during which we had forged steadily, though slowly along, meeting with no further incident, when we suddenly came into a sort of field that seemed well equipped with trees. One of us kicked something that rolled in the grass and which when found, proved to be an apple. We were in an orchard, but we found that there wasn't a single tree whose branches could be reached from the ground and we were far too weak to climb, so we started to search for wind-blown fruit. In this we met with little success, (which was perhaps little to be expected, considering that the orchard would be over-run with German soldiers during the day time), but here and there we came upon occasional apples, small, and hard, as we groped around in the darkness.

Suddenly I realised that my partner was no longer with me. We had been so intent in our search for the fruit, that we had drifted apart and I began to get a little agitated, as there was a big chance of our straying completely out of touch with each other and I was as much concerned on his behalf as on my own. I daren't risk calling out, because situated as we were now, it might have had more than the desired effect. So, I remained where I was standing in the hope that White would work his way back again.

Many minutes passed by without result and I was just beginning to get alarmed when a sudden football on the grass behind me caused me to turn round with a feeling of relief, to greet the return of my partner. This feeling died on the instant when the approaching figure came near enough for me to make out the figure of a German soldier, complete with shrapnel helmet.

Paralysed with astonishment and sudden fright, I was unable to move and all manner of wild things chased through my mind as the man walked up to where I stood. I was just going to risk all in a wild swipe with the heavy stick I was carrying, when the man spoke and I got another shock, because the voice was unmistakably that of my partner.

The mental strain I had undergone during the last few minutes made me quite faint and sick for a moment or two and when I felt alright again I told White of the fright he had unwittingly given me. Realising how it must have appeared to me, he fell immediately to apologising and cursing his thoughtlessness.

He had picked up the helmet a short distance away and without thinking, had clapped it on his head, it being a welcome acquisition, both as a covering, and as a protection against the shrapnel we would have to reckon with later on. However, I was quite relieved to find that things were as they were and we set out on the forward move again, leaving the orchard where we had spent more than an hour of valuable time in the gathering of less than a dozen tiny apples.

CHAPTER 20

As we tramped along we came upon shell holes of recent creation and we began to experience the old thrills of being in the line again. The reports of firing guns and exploding shells were only a mile or two in front of us and we knew that if it were possible for us to walk ahead in a straight line for an hour, we would be among our own troops.

For all that, however, the goal still seemed a great way off when we remembered that the German Army lay between and that there were two curtains of Artillery fire and rifle fire to pass through before we could consider ourselves safe and free again.

Our next halt was in a field cultivated of wheat and there was even now a fair amount of growing corn, wild sewn from the previous year, in it. This was mostly ruined, as many shells had exploded among it and blasted it down in every direction. We filled our pockets with wheat grains, (doing the separating by rubbing the heads of corn between the palms of our hands, to obviate the carrying of even the smallest thing that would be of no use to us), which, with the few apples gathered earlier, solved the food question for us.

Working our way out of the field, we found ourselves back on the road and noticed on it and around it the signs of frequent attention from the allied artillery. The road was deserted save for ourselves and we went on a little way until we came on a natural trench standing away to the right. We made our way along this for about 20 yards and came to a deep dug-out sunk down into the right bank of the trench which obviously, from the direction in which the entrance faced, had been dug, and used by the French when they had used this part of the front.

The night was almost ended and it was about time we got into hiding again, so we started to explore the sap. It was some time before we could bring ourselves to the point of entering, because there was the possibility of it being used and occupied by the troops, but at last, after convincing ourselves that none of the enemy would use a dug-out with the entrance facing the wrong direction, we ventured in.

Quite a number of steps led down into the dug-out and at the foot of these an old blanket which had served for a gas curtain was still hanging. We found no one inside the dug-out itself, which had never been completed, the timber finishing at the foot of the steps. When we passed beyond the blanket we found just a hole in the clay about 6 feet square, with the same for height, and that made us feel a little more safe though it promised an uncomfortable day for us. However, stretching ourselves out on the clay floor, which was strewn with reeds, we covered ourselves with our priceless blanket and settled down to make the most of what our latest hiding place had to afford for our rest, after first lighting one of the candles which we had acquired, when raiding the kit boxes four nights previously. We hadn't required them, (or been able to use them), before. We were quite safe in using them now because we had ascertained that the light would not penetrate the blanket and as we should hear the attempt of anyone descending the stairs, we would be able to put out the light before it could be noticed.

Then we made a meal of two or three apples and some wheat, lit up the last remaining of our cigars, taking alternate puffs of it, and discussed the position. At the present stage we reckoned ourselves to be near the light field gun positions and the support trenches, (that we were entering the active zone was emphasized by the occasional report, which came to our ears 30 feet below the earth's surface as a dull, heavy thud of a shell bursting in the vicinity; it felt strange to be under the fire of our own side), so our next move should take us, if our luck held, to the front line trenches.

The time had come to make our final plans and this we commenced to do in sublime optimism, if it were only the matter of covering the distance that counted.

We were both at the end of our tether, (to make matters worse, our boots had completely given out and I was walking on the bare soles of my feet) and we decided that the next move must see the end of our journey whatever happened. Should we have the good fortune to reach the enemy's firing trench without interference, we would creep out to the wire entanglements, find the gap used by scout patrols, and raiding parties, rest near the gap until a favourable opportunity arose and we felt equal to the dash, and then take our chance against the fire of both sides in an attempt to reach our own trenches.

Of one thing we were certain. It just <u>had</u> to be the next night, because we would be dead from hunger before another night came round.

When we had completed the arrangements as far as was possible to make them, we settled down to what we hoped was our last day's rest in the enemy's territory. We put out the cigar when a little more than half of it had been burnt, to save the butt for a final smoke before setting out again and dousing the candle we wished ourselves all the luck to take ourselves safely through the last stage. We then fell asleep, huddled close together for warmth, as the uncovered walls of the dug-out struck damp, and cold.

CHAPTER 21

It might have been any time of the day when we awoke again, and it wasn't advisable to leave the shelter of the dug-out, because lifting the gas curtain and crawling part of the way up the steps we could see that it was daylight outside, so we settled ourselves for a tedious wait for nightfall again. Further sleep was out of the question. For one thing we were far too excited now that we were near our objective and for another, we still needed to be alert in case anyone should visit our hiding place.

It required a great deal of patience to remain lying down for hours, with nothing to do to help pass the time; not even a scrap of paper to read, (except the tattered service pay book in my pocket, to which I had tenaciously clung when everything else had gone and which I had examined many times since capture) and with both of us too weary even to talk.

However, on one or two occasions there occurred breaks in the monotony when a German soldier would come down the steps of our dug-out, only to retreat when we made sounds to inform him the place was occupied. Though each one spoke, none of them descended as far as the curtain; not even the last one, who gave us most cause for alarm, and even yet it seems hard to believe our luck in this respect.

A little heavy shelling in the immediate vicinity was responsible for the appearance of our last visitor, who apparently came down for shelter. Stopping before the curtain, he called out as the others had done and receiving a grunt in reply, similar to those returned in the previous cases, he asked a question, evidently with the object of learning the designation of our regiment, because he mentioned two or three branches before I thought it advisable when he reached "FLEMMENWERFER" to supply a muffled "JA". He seemed in no hurry to go away, because we could hear him squat down on the stairs, after which he made a few conversational remarks at intervals, some of them connected with the shelling that was going on outside. The grunts that he received in answer must have given him the idea that all was not well with us, because he started to enquire after our health; at least he used a word that sounded like "KRANKEN" in one of his questions and even my scanty knowledge of German told me that the word meant "hurt" or "sick". I heaved up a realistic groan to strengthen the idea. That settled it. Our visitor didn't say another word during the rest of the time he remained sitting on the stairs, (which would probably be an hour), except to utter some farewell remark when at last he decided to get moving.

After several stealthy trips up the stairs to see how the night was advancing, (and daylight seemed to fade very slowly that day), we eventually decided that it was dark enough to travel, so we made another meal on wheat and sour apples, smoked our last piece of cigar, sharing the whiffs until it was quite finished, and quit the dug-out, leaving behind the blanket that had served us so well during our journey.

There was no moon, but the sky was thickly dotted with stars that provided sufficient illumination to enable us to make out things 20 or 30 yards away.

With every sense alert, we stepped steadily along, following no particular track, but heading straight for the occasional "Verey" lights. These became plainer as we advanced and we knew that soon we would need to drop to cover whenever the light went up. There were sounds of men moving about near at hand, but we were managing to keep out of their way. After a time we came to a sunken road in a rather wide and shallow valley and on the sides of the further bank we could make out dug-outs. A light railway track ran through the valley, but nothing was moving along it. Crossing the valley, we avoided the dug-outs and passed over the far bank, coming on to what seemed a tract of fairly level plain.

We hadn't moved far over this before there came evidence that we had been seen. Someone was shouting behind us and turning round, we made out the figure of a man about 40 yards away slowly making his way towards us. Increasing our pace to a fast walk we carried straight on, with the intention of attempting a little run when we had succeeded in putting enough distance between us to make sight indistinct and gradually we drew away from the man in the rear who kept on following us and occasionally calling out. It may have been that he himself was lost and was expecting us to guide him, (that was the idea we had later), but whatever he was we daren't risk his catching us up and at last we succeeded in shaking him off.

CHAPTER 22

A little later we came to the first line of barbed wire which told us that we were in the region of the support trenches. The wire wasn't thickly woven and we didn't have much trouble in getting over, though my bare soles got cut about a little.

By now we were in front of the enemy artillery fire, having apparently passed the field batteries, (which must have been in the vicinity of the sunken road) and occasional shells bound for the Allies lines whistled over our heads.

Advancing more warily now, we continued our forward march toward the ever nearing lights, until we stopped just short of pitching headlong into a pit that yawned suddenly in front of us. It was a machine gun emplacement and the gunner immediately challenged us. We didn't answer, but skirting the emplacement we bore right off to the left and crouched ready to drop at the first sign of a burst from the gun. However, this wasn't coming, as the challenge was answered by someone, evidently an Officer coming over from the right to inspect the position, because we heard him drop into the pit. We didn't wait for any more, but headed for a dark patch which proved to be a swamp with a dense growth of reeds that reached well above our heads. For some minutes we had been aware of a dull red glow in the distance and it was towards this that we steered our way through the reeds, moving slowly, and with the utmost caution to keep down the sounds of our movements, because we were reckoning ourselves to be near the front line now.

At last we came to the edge of the marsh, only to find to our dismay that a river some 15 to 20 yards wide lay in front of us. Beyond the far bank were the ruins of a large village or small town, which lay on the side of a rising slope. The lower houses were in flames, which accounted for the glow in the sky we had seen.

We searched about for some means of crossing the river, knowing that there was no chance of finding a bridge standing and eventually we came across a series of stepping stones formed of a quantity of old casks, cases, and other junk. There were large gaps between some of the items and it meant jumping for it now and then and chancing the floating rubbish to be sufficiently buoyant to remain floating under our weight. Gingerly putting a foot on the first cask, I found it apparently sound and with White starting from another point, we essayed the tricky crossing.

I had managed to get half way across the river when a solid looking packing case, on which I had just stepped, suddenly sunk under my weight, and I immediately followed it below the surface. As I came up again, gasping and spluttering, and in a real panic, (having discovered that the river was far too deep at that point for me to reach the bottom), I let out a wild yell to my partner before going under again. Then something seemed to flare up inside me. Perhaps I went temporarily mad through the knowledge that I had succeeded in coming right through the nerve racking ordeal we had undergone for nearly a week, only to be drowned like a rat almost within arms-reach of our own front line and freedom.

Anyway, the next thing I realised when my senses came back was that I was clinging to the bank at the far side, gasping for breath, and with a stomach full of the vile tasting water of the river, whilst my partner lay flat on the bank, holding me up by the arms and vainly trying to lift me out of the water. I had never swum a stroke in my life previously, but in some unaccountable manner I had managed to force myself across ten or twelve yards of this river.

With the feeling that I was just coming out of some horrible nightmare I hung there while the breath came painfully back to my lungs, both of us afraid to move as we realised that the disturbance caused may have given the alarm to some of the enemy. However, nothing occurred to indicate this and at last, after a mighty effort on both our parts, I struggled out onto the bank, where I lay for some minutes shivering with cold, and vomiting up the filthy water of the river

When I felt strong enough to stand, we made for the first of the burning houses, only one wall of which remained standing, with the flames eating their way over it. There was no sign of a trench anywhere, yet we were evidently in No-Man's Land because shells from both sides were dropping within a restricted radius of which the ground we were standing on formed the centre. Machine gun and rifle bullets from both directions were whistling past us too and gradually realisation came to us that the armies were engaged in a running fight, in which there was no chance for either side to fully consolidate their positions. It was also evident that the town had only recently been subjected to the bombardment that had shattered it and that the fires had but lately occurred.

The ruined town presented a weird appearance as we viewed it in the half light of approaching dawn, standing in front of the blazing wall to dry and warm ourselves. The thought of drawing rifle or machine gun fire upon us as we stood there with figures thrown up in clear relief by the flames never troubled us in the least. We had arrived at the stage when movement and thought had become mechanical and it was beyond the power of anything to give us further shocks.

When the heat of the flames had partly driven the chill from us, we set out to work our way up the street, keeping close to the side as caution returned to us. From the fact that our own shells were dropping at least 20 yards behind us, we gathered that our own lines must be right near. The street inclined steadily and in the dim light we guessed it to be 50 or 60 yards to the crest. Once over the crest and it was practically certain that we must be among our own people, so on we went, too weak to achieve more than a slow, staggering walk.

We were within 15 or 20 yards of the crest and still unable to see over it, when we heard the sounds made by the cautious approach of a small party of troops from the other side of it. Assuming this to be a returning enemy patrol or raiding party we quickly glanced round for a place to hide and found, right alongside, a tunnel-like opening that was evidently the entrance to a cellar. We stepped into the passage, which was totally void of light, and as we groped our way inside, (taking care not to penetrate too far in case the cellar should prove to be occupied by the enemy), the footsteps came nearer. Then, to our consternation and dismay, we heard voices at the far end of the passage and sounds made by someone coming out. We retreated slowly to the entrance again, in the hope that the men coming down the street would pass before we were driven out, but again we were baulked. Just as we reached the entrance, with the men that were leaving the cellar close on our heels, the party, numbering about 4 or 5, came abreast.

We had no chance but to risk all in a sudden dash into the street, lay on with our sticks if anyone intercepted us, and use the last of our strength in a spurt for the other side of the crest, if there was an opportunity provided. Failing this, we could only go down kicking – as we would in any case, if we remained where we were.

Reaching the street at the same moment as the men passed the entrance, we heard them talking softly among themselves and I could hardly believe my ears when I caught phrases in English, with the unmistakeable American accent. My eyes straining through the half-light made out the familiar type of shrapnel helmet worn by the Allies – and then I did a very foolish thing.

Running straight out at one of them, I threw my arms round his neck and commenced babbling in hysterical relief, burbling out all sorts of stuff in the attempt to tell him who we were. The unfortunate soldier, startled out of his wits, let out a yell, and struggled wildly to free himself and bring his rifle and bayonet into action.

His comrades, alarmed no less than he by the sudden apparition at such a place and such an hour, were already travelling back up the street as quickly as their legs would carry them.

Coming sharply to my senses to realise the extent of the mischief caused and the likelihood of a bayonet thrust from the man I had so violently scared, I shifted my hands to the muzzle of his rifle as it came up and held it like grim death, he cursing and trying to wrench it free, while I desperately tried to make him understand that I was British and a friend, before he could succeed in doing so.

Our hosts soon turned out some food for us and we soon engaged in disposing of the first real meal since being captured and the first food for three or four days. Though there was plenty of it and plenty of time in which to eat it, we gulped it down like ravenous beasts, more than half afraid that we would be torn from it before we could satisfy the torturing hunger that was resultant from such a lengthy period of starvation. Between us we succeeded in clearing up two 16 oz cans of salmon and a large quantity of the light bread peculiar to the American commissariat – disregarding the warnings of our hosts that it might be dangerous to eat heavily in our wasted condition. As a result we made ourselves too ill to stand.

The Americans had apologised for not being able to supply us with anything better in the way of food, but they got some idea of the godsend it had been to us when we told them that we hadn't even seen anything like it for months. To add a little weight to our story, I took from the pocket of my wet and ragged dungaree trousers what had been expected to form our total sustenance for that day – a small handful of wheat grains, reduced to a sticky mass by their immersion in the river.

CHAPTER 23

While we rested to pick up a little strength so that we could be conducted behind the lines and smoked real cigarettes again, supplied in abundance by our rescuers, they told us many things about the position of affairs on our side, going right back to the time we had ceased to be conversant with them. It was good to be able to talk again on common subjects that had been strange to us.

We learnt that the ruins that we were at present in the midst of had been the town of FISMES, (the river in which we had fallen overnight and had the vile water which I had swallowed in such a generous quantity, was the VESLE), and the Americans had only come up during the last few days after chasing the enemy back from CHATEAU THIERRY. Neither side had had time to construct a proper firing trench and we had walked right through the machine gun nests with which the enemy was defending his front.

It came as great news to us that our own army were also doing great things and the Germans were being steadily pushed back at every point – which bore out the conviction I had acquired during my last three or four days in the compound.

When we first entered the cellar and had our "particulars" taken, a runner had been sent off to the Company Headquarters with the information. He eventually returned with the instructions that we were to be taken behind to Divisional Headquarters as soon as possible for examination. Accordingly, as soon as we had gained sufficient strength to attempt the journey, (which wasn't long, because we were naturally eager to get back to civilisation and health), we set out to cross the shell-pitted ground lying between the runs and the support lines, escorted by one of the Officers.

We had a rather stormy passage, it being now daylight and the country under clear observation by the enemy. In addition to the general activity of machine guns and artillery, a sniping field gun kept dropping a shell right behind our heels at intervals of about a minute. Somehow we didn't seem to worry a bit – we were back among our friends and that caused such a wonderful feeling of safety and immunity that had the entire German artillery been concentrated on that point, I don't think we would have experienced panic or increased our pace in the slightest.

Eventually we passed out of the zone covered by the light field guns and small arms and came to the supports, where we rested awhile with dozens of Americans, flocking around us to hear our yarn, loading us with dozens of cigarettes, while a genial and big hearted cook feasted us with bacon and beans and coffee.

Before we left the cellar, the Officer suggested that it would perhaps be well if we discarded our German headgear as it might cause a misunderstanding among the soldiers we would meet, (this was a sound idea which was readily appreciated by us – remembering the fright I had had in the orchard and the scare we had unwillingly given the soldiers in the darkened street that morning) and we soon saw the reason for this. The "Doughboys" were evidently bitter against the Germans and there were some threatening moves toward us as we approached the men in the support lines, which instantly changed to cheery welcome when it was discovered who were really were and their bitterness was expressed in big oaths as they took in our ghastly condition.

After a pleasant rest of about an hour, during which our new friends couldn't do enough for our comfort, showering things upon us, and generally making a tremendous fuss of us, a motor cycle and side car came up to take us down to Divisional Headquarters some miles behind.

Arriving there we were questioned by Staff Officers, to whom we were able to supply a lot of useful information concerning the immediate front and the country behind it. They were very nice to us, giving us more cigarettes and ensuring that we were comfortable and after obtaining the information they needed, they sent us down to Corps Headquarters by car.

This was some miles away and we were glad when the ride came to an end, as the sun was very fierce and this being the first time we had been out in daylight for a week, we found the bright light extremely painful to the eyes.

We arrived at Corps Headquarters sometime in the afternoon and after a brief questioning were sent to be cleansed, clothed, and fed, after which we could take a rest before presenting ourselves for an interview with the Corps Commander. For this we were put in the charge of the Provost-Marshal's staff and they made a thorough job of it too. White and I stood in wooden wash-tubs whilst two husky big policemen scrubbed us down with fibre scrubbing brushes. Our evil-smelling old rags were taken away from us and we were clipped and shaved and fitted out with American uniforms, after which we were given a meal of such a tempting nature and variety that 24 hours before it would have been risking our sanity to <u>think</u> about it.

Rested, (and feeling better already – although the strain was beginning to tell on us), we were taken before the Corps Commander and his staff, to whom we gave all the information in our possession.

The following day we were claimed by the French and were taken to the Headquarters of the 6th Army at CHATEAU THIERRY, on the MARNE, where we were billeted with a regiment of Chasseurs d'Alpin.

Working round about the billets were a number of German prisoners and we bitterly noted the contrast in conditions between them and those unfortunate ones of ours we had lately left.

We stayed at the 6th Army H.Q. for three or four days, during which an interpreter, (a Staff Officer of some rank), was often in attendance upon us, though the first job of this kindly person was to push through a cable to the relatives of White and myself, to let them know that we were alive and safe.

Unfortunately the French style of feeding is extremely difficult for a British person to get accustomed to, (even if he be in good health) and though the food they gave us was excellent in quality and generous in quantity, the nature of the meals proved too much for us. White collapsed after a couple of days and had to be taken to hospital where he spent some time before he was well enough to proceed home.

At last my request to be sent home, (which had been sympathetically received but returned with regretful excuses by the interpreter), was granted. However, when I got to CHATEAU THIERRY railway station on the afternoon I was to leave, the train was packed with such a crown of soldiers going up to Paris on short leave, that there wasn't room left for a cat to squeeze into and the interpreter, (who seemed to have acquired solicitous interest and care of a father for me), suggested that I go back and wait for the next train – two days. This I refused to do and announced my intention of travelling on the roof of the carriage. At first the interpreter would not hear of this, but when a small party of American soldiers undertook to look after me he agreed to let me go and we made the journey to Paris on the roof of the train.

Arriving at the Gare du Nord, I made my way to the Pepiniere Barracks, being billeted there for two days until I had put in a few more interviews with Intelligence Officers, etc, after which I was despatched to ETAPLES. From there I was sent to MONTREUIL, the Headquarters of the Commander in Chief of the British Army, and after another interview, was fitted out with a British soldier's uniform and sent to England.

A few more days spent in interviews at various departments, during which time I was billeted with the Scots Guards at Wellington Barracks, and I was allowed to proceed home, where good food and kindly attention worked wonders with me and where, safe in the knowledge that I was back again among friends, I slowly recovered from an experience that even now at times stands out like a vivid nightmare.

THE END

Mark Pennock-Purvis in 1972

Printed in Great Britain
by Amazon